Little Pebble™

Staying Safe

School Bus Safety

by Sarah L. Schuette

Consultant: Shonette Doggett, coalition coordinator
Safe Kids Greater East Metro/St. Croix Valley
St. Paul, Minnesota

PEBBLE
a capstone imprint

Little Pebble is published by Pebble
1710 Roe Crest Drive
North Mankato, Minnesota 56003
www.mycapstone.com

Library of Congress Cataloging-in-Publication Data
Names: Schuette, Sarah L., 1976– author.
Title: School bus safety / by Sarah L. Schuette.
Description: North Mankato, Minnesota : Pebble, a
Capstone imprint, [2020] | Series: Little Pebble. Staying
safe! | Audience: Age 6–8. | Audience: K to Grade
3. | Includes bibliographical references and index.
Identifiers: LCCN 2018052365| ISBN 9781977108715
(hardcover) | ISBN 9781977110312 (pbk.) | ISBN
9781977108791 (ebook pdf) Subjects: LCSH: School
buses—Safety measures—Juvenile literature. | School
children—Transportation—Safety measures. | CYAC:
School buses—Safety measures. | School children—
Transportation—Safety measures. | LCGFT: Instructional
and educational works. Classification: LCC LB2864 .S39
2020 | DDC 371.8/72—dc23
LC record available at https://lccn.loc.gov/2018052365

Editorial Credits

Erika L. Shores, editor; Heidi Thompson, designer;
Morgan Walters, media researcher; Marcy Morin,
scheduler; Tori Abraham, production specialist

Photo Credits

All photos by Capstone Studio/Karon Dubke

All internet sites appearing in back matter were available
and accurate when this book was sent to press.

The author dedicates this book to her school bus driver,
Joe Bertrang, Henderson, Minnesota.

Printed and bound in China.
001671

Table of Contents

At the Bus Stop

Dev walks to the bus stop.

He waits three big steps
from the curb.

Here is the bus.

Dev waits for the doors

to open.

WATCH YOUR STEP

9

Riding the Bus

Get on!

Dev holds on to

the railings.

ENTRANCE
DOOR
RELEASE

STEP

Dev stays in his seat.

He holds his bag.

He might put it under
his seat.

Dev follows the rules.

He does not yell.

The bus stops.

Dev waits his turn.

Riders in front get off first.

Dev crosses in front of the bus. He stays 10 big steps away. The driver needs to see him.

Stay Safe on the Bus

Dev knows the bus rules.

Thanks for a safe ride!

Glossary

bus stop—a place where people wait for the bus

curb—the edge between a street and a sidewalk or path

railing—a handle by the steps of a bus

rule—an instruction telling people what to do; rules help people stay safe

Read More

Hicks, Dwayne. *Rules on the School Bus.* Rules at School. New York: PowerKids Press, 2020.

Rustad, Martha E. H. *Tanya Takes the School Bus.* Off to School. Minneapolis: Millbrook Press, 2018.

Schuh, Mari C. *Buses: A 4D Book.* Transportation. North Mankato, MN: Capstone, 2019.

Internet Sites

Safety Dog
www.firststudentinc.com/why-first-student/
safety-dog

School Bus and School Zone Safety Kids Page
www.safeny.ny.gov/Kids/kid-schl.htm#top

Super-cool stuff!

Check out projects, games, and lots more at
www.capstonekids.com

Critical Thinking Questions

1. How far should you stand from the curb while you wait for the bus?

2. What do you do when crossing in front of the bus?

3. What might be some reasons why you should not yell on the bus?

Index